Content Marketing That Sells: How to Attract Customers by Communicating Value

Copyright © 2024 Reginaldo Osnildo
All rights reserved.

PRESENTATION

INTRODUCTION TO CONTENT MARKETING

UNDERSTANDING YOUR TARGET AUDIENCE

STRATEGIC CONTENT PLANNING

TYPES OF CONTENT THAT CONVERT

CREATING HIGH QUALITY CONTENT

SEO FOR CONTENT

PERSUASIVE WRITING

STORYTELLING IN CONTENT

CONTENT OPTIMIZATION AND FORMATTING

CONTENT DISTRIBUTION

CONTENT MARKETING ON SOCIAL MEDIA

MEASURING CONTENT SUCCESS

LEAD GENERATION WITH CONTENT

CONTENT REPURPOSING

ENGAGEMENT AND INTERACTION

USE OF IMAGES AND VIDEOS

CONTENT FOR EMAIL MARKETING

BUILDING COMMUNITY THROUGH CONTENT

COMMON CHALLENGES IN CONTENT MARKETING

CONTENT AND CONVERSION

AUTHENTICITY AND TRANSPARENCY

FUTURE OF CONTENT MARKETING

RESOURCES AND TOOLS FOR CONTENT CREATORS

CREATING A CONTENT LEGACY

REGINALDO OSNILDO

PRESENTATION

Welcome to " **Content Marketing That Sells: How to Attract Customers by Communicating Value** ," your definitive guide to turning every word into a powerful customer magnet. If you are a marketer, entrepreneur or content creator, this book was made especially for you, thinking about your daily needs and challenges. With the digital world constantly evolving, it has never been more essential to master the art of creating and utilizing content that not only attracts, but effectively converts visitors into loyal, engaged customers.

In this book, you'll discover tried-and-true strategies for developing, executing, and measuring a content marketing strategy tailored for today. Through the following pages, I will share not only the theory behind each technique, but also practical insights that will help you apply them directly in your everyday life. Prepared to synthesize knowledge, provide innovation and facilitate your journey towards success, this book is an invitation for you to revolutionize the way your content impacts the world.

With a direct and results-focused approach, each chapter has been carefully designed so that, at the end of your reading, you will have in your hands a complete arsenal of tools to attract, engage and convert. With each topic covered, you will be equipped with the necessary knowledge to make the content a true sales force, understanding not only the "how", but the "why" of each strategy being effective.

This is not just another book about content marketing. It is your new ally on the journey of transforming information into real value for your customers and, consequently, into tangible growth for your business or project. With rich and engaging content, each page of this book is prepared to be a step on the ladder of your success.

I invite you now to dive into the first chapter, where we will explore the basics of content marketing. Get ready to discover why this powerful marketing tool continues to be indispensable in attracting and converting customers, and how you can start applying it effectively now.

The journey to mastering content marketing starts here. Let's together uncover the secrets of creating content that not only captures attention, but wins hearts and minds, guaranteeing results that speak for themselves. Come, the next chapter awaits you.

Yours sincerely

Reginaldo Osnildo

INTRODUCTION TO CONTENT MARKETING

In today's digital universe, content marketing stands out as one of the most powerful and essential tools for any professional who wants to not only reach, but engage and convert their audience into loyal customers. In this chapter, you will understand what content marketing is and why it is so vital in the current context of business and digital communication.

WHAT IS CONTENT MARKETING?

Content marketing is a marketing strategy focused on creating and distributing relevant, valuable, and consistent content to attract and retain a clearly defined target audience — and, ultimately, to drive profitable customer action. Unlike other forms of advertising, content marketing focuses less on direct sales and more on establishing a relationship of trust with the consumer, positioning your brand as a reference in the sector.

WHY CONTENT MARKETING?

1. **Increases your brand's visibility:** Every piece of content you create is an opportunity to be seen and recognized in the market.
2. **Builds lasting relationships with your audience:** Valuable content builds trust, establishing an emotional connection with your audience that goes beyond commercial transactions.
3. **Improves positioning in search engines:** Well-planned and optimized content can increase your position in search results, attracting more organic traffic to your website.
4. **Generates leads and drives conversions:** By educating your audience about your products or services in a subtle and effective way, content makes the sales process more fluid and natural.
5. **It's a long-term investment:** Unlike advertising campaigns that have a limited lifespan, quality content can continue to attract and engage for months or years

after its creation.

UPDATE OF CONCEPTS FOR TODAY

In a world where the amount of information available is overwhelming, the quality of the content you produce has never been more crucial. You need to not only capture your audience's attention, but keep it, ensuring that every interaction with your brand adds value. This means creating content that is not just informative, but engaging and inspiring, something that truly resonates with your audience's needs and desires.

MAKING READERS' LIFE EASIER

This book is designed to make your learning and application of content marketing concepts as easy as possible. Each strategy and technique presented here is accompanied by practical examples and applicable tips, so you can start implementing what you learn right away, seeing tangible results as quickly as possible.

By completing this chapter, I hope you have a clear and in-depth understanding of why content marketing should be a key part of your digital marketing strategy. In the next chapter, we'll dive into how you can accurately understand your target audience, creating the foundation for all the content work that follows.

UNDERSTANDING YOUR TARGET AUDIENCE

Mastering content marketing starts with a fundamental step: deeply knowing who your target audience is. This chapter is dedicated to exploring how you can identify and understand your audience so that the content you create truly resonates with them, capturing their attention and building lasting loyalty.

IDENTIFICATION OF THE TARGET AUDIENCE

First of all, it is crucial to define who the people you want to reach are. This involves understanding not only basic demographics like age, gender, and location, but also diving deeper into psychographics like interests, values, and behaviors.

1. **Demographic analysis:** Start by collecting basic data that describes your audience. Tools like Google Analytics and social media offer valuable insights into who are already interested in your content.
2. **Psychographic study:** Understand what motivates your audience. Surveys, focus groups, and direct feedback are effective methods for capturing their preferences, motivations, and objections.
3. **Audience segmentation:** Based on the information collected, segment your audience into smaller groups with specific needs and interests. This allows for more personalized and effective content creation.

CREATING PERSONAS

Once you have a clear understanding of who your audience is, the next step is to create personas. Personas are semi-fictional representations of your ideal customer, based on real data about your existing customers and market research. They help visualize your audience as real individuals, making it easier to create content that speaks directly to their wants and needs.

1. **details :** Include details in your persona such as name, occupation, challenges, and how your product or service fits into their life.

2. **Using personas:** Use these personas to guide all content creation decisions. Ask yourself: "Would this solve a problem for my persona? Would it engage them?"

APPLYING AUDIENCE KNOWLEDGE TO CONTENT

With in-depth knowledge of your audience, you are now in a position to create content that not only catches their attention, but is also valued by them. That includes:

1. **Targeted content:** Develop themes and messages that directly address your personas' interests and needs.
2. **Tone and style:** Adapt the tone and style of your content to speak directly to your audience. If your audience is more formal, a serious tone may be better. If it is a younger and more dynamic audience, a more informal and energetic style may be more effective.
3. **Continuous feedback:** Maintain an open channel of communication with your audience to continue learning and adjusting your approach as needed.

By the end of this chapter, I hope you feel more equipped to not just know, but understand and connect with your audience on a deeper, more meaningful level. In the next chapter, we'll build on this solid foundation by diving into the steps to developing an effective content strategy that perfectly aligns with your business goals.

STRATEGIC CONTENT PLANNING

Once you understand who your target audience is and what they're looking for, the next step is to develop a strategic content plan that not only meets those needs, but also supports your business's overall goals. This chapter will guide you through the crucial steps for creating a robust and effective content strategy that will ensure that each piece of content contributes meaningfully to your marketing goals.

DEFINITION OF CONTENT OBJECTIVES

Before anything else, it is essential to clearly define what objectives you want to achieve with your content. These goals can range from increasing brand awareness, generating leads, improving conversion rate, to gaining customer loyalty. Having clear and measurable objectives is essential to guide your actions and measure the success of your content strategy.

CUSTOMER JOURNEY MAPPING

Understanding the customer journey is crucial to creating content that is relevant and timely. You must identify the different stages your customer goes through, from discovery to purchasing decision and beyond, so you can create content that smoothly guides them through each phase.

1. **Awareness:** Content that informs the public about a problem they may not know they have.
2. **Consideration:** Content that helps your audience evaluate how your brand or products can solve their problems.
3. **Decision:** Content that convinces the audience that your solution is the best option.
4. **Retention:** Content that keeps existing customers engaged and satisfied with your brand.

CREATION OF THE EDITORIAL CALENDAR

An editorial calendar is an indispensable tool in content planning. It helps organize the production and publication of your content, ensuring balanced and consistent distribution over time. Here are some steps to create your calendar:

1. **Plan ahead:** Define themes and content formats for the coming months, considering important dates and industry events.
2. **Diversify formats:** Include a variety of content types, such as blog posts, videos, podcasts, and infographics, to keep your audience interested.
3. **Assign responsibilities:** Make it clear who is responsible for creating, reviewing, and publishing each piece of content.

MONITORING AND ADJUSTMENT

Strategic content planning is not a static process; You need to constantly monitor the performance of your content and make adjustments as needed. Use analytics tools to track how your content is performing against your goals and make adjustments to optimize your strategy.

By the end of this chapter, you should have a solid understanding of how to strategically plan your content so that it effectively meets your business goals and the needs of your audience. In the next chapter, we'll explore the different types of content you can use to capture your prospects' attention and encourage them to move forward in their buying journey.

TYPES OF CONTENT THAT CONVERT

Now that you're equipped with a solid content strategy and a clear understanding of your audience and goals, it's time to explore the different types of content you can use to attract and convert customers. This chapter provides an overview of the most effective content formats in digital marketing and how each can be used to maximize your results.

BLOGS

Blog posts are one of the most traditional forms of marketing content, but they continue to be extremely effective. They are ideal for improving your SEO, educating your audience on relevant topics, and establishing your brand as an authority in your niche.

- **How to use:** Create blog posts that address your audience's most common questions and problems. Use a style that reflects your brand voice and include calls to action (CTAs) that guide readers to the next step.

VIDEOS

Video content is growing in popularity and effectiveness. Videos can be used to demonstrate products, explain complex concepts in an accessible way, and connect with audiences in a more personal and direct way.

- **How to use:** Develop tutorial videos, product demonstrations, or interviews with experts. Make sure videos are optimized for mobile, as many users access video content through mobile devices.

INFOGRAPHICS

Infographics are powerful tools for presenting data and statistics in a visual, easily digestible way. They are perfect for attracting attention on social media platforms and your own website.

- **How to use:** Use infographics to summarize relevant research, show advances in your industry, or explain how your products or services work. They're also useful for sharing in blog posts or newsletters.

E-BOOKS AND WHITEPAPERS

E-books and whitepapers are excellent for lead generation because they allow you to delve deeper into a specific topic, offering great value to your audience in exchange for their contact information.

- **How to use:** Offer e-books or whitepapers as a free download on your website, requiring interested parties to provide their email and perhaps other information to access them. This helps build your email list and nurture leads.

PODCASTS

Podcasts are an effective way to reach an audience that prefers auditory content and are perfect for discussing topics in-depth, building a community, and establishing a personal connection with listeners.

- **How to use it:** Launch a podcast series covering important issues in your industry or interviewing other experts. Promote your episodes on your social media and other content platforms.

INTERACTIVE CONTENT

Quizzes, calculators and games are forms of interactive content that can increase engagement and provide a personalized user experience.

- **How to Use:** Integrate interactive content on your website to educate your audience, gather insights into their preferences, and encourage them to interact more with your brand.

By the end of this chapter, you should have a broad overview of the types of content that can be used in your marketing strategy to effectively attract and convert. Each format has its role and, when used correctly, can bring significant results to your company.

In the next chapter, we'll delve deeper into how to create high-quality content that not only attracts, but deeply engages your audience, taking your brand to the next level.

CREATING HIGH QUALITY CONTENT

The quality of the content you produce can define the success or failure of your digital marketing strategy. In this chapter, we'll explore essential techniques for creating content that not only attracts but is also valuable and engaging, elevating your brand and building trust with your audience.

UNDERSTANDING THE CONCEPT OF VALUE

High-quality content is content that delivers real value to your readers, listeners or viewers. This means each piece of content must:

1. **Solve a problem:** Be it informational, emotional or practical.
2. **Be relevant:** It must meet the current needs and interests of the public.
3. **Be trustworthy:** Rely on verified information and present an authoritative perspective.

HIGH QUALITY CONTENT ELEMENTS

To ensure your content is high quality, consider the following elements:

1. **Originality:** Avoid repeating what has already been said. Offer new perspectives or unique insights.
2. **Clarity and precision:** Communicate clearly and directly, without ambiguity.
3. **Engagement:** Use language that speaks directly to your audience, with a tone that resonates with them.
4. **Visually appealing:** Include visual elements, such as images and videos, to complement and reinforce your message.
5. **Action-oriented:** Include clear calls to action that guide users on what to do next.

CONTENT PRODUCTION PROCESS

Creating high-quality content requires a systematic, well-planned process. Here are the steps to follow:

1. **Research and planning:** Start with detailed research into the topic, including understanding the issues most relevant to your audience.
2. **Writing the first draft:** With the information collected, write a first draft, focusing on delivering all the important information without initially worrying about writing perfection.
3. **Review and editing:** Refine your draft, improving the clarity and flow of the text, ensuring the content is engaging and easy to understand.
4. **SEO Optimization:** Make sure the content is optimized for search engines, using relevant keywords without compromising the naturalness of the text.
5. **Feedback:** If possible, get feedback from colleagues or members of the public before final publication.

KEEPING CONSISTENCY

Consistency is key to maintaining quality and building a trustworthy brand. This includes maintaining a consistent voice across all of your content and posting regularly to keep your audience engaged and informed.

By the end of this chapter, you should have the tools and knowledge necessary to start producing high-quality content that not only attracts but also retains the attention of your audience, establishing your brand as a reference in the market.

In the next chapter, we'll explore how you can utilize SEO principles to ensure your content is not only high-quality, but also easily found by search engines.

SEO FOR CONTENT

Search engine optimization, or SEO, is essential to ensuring that your content is found by those looking for relevant information online. This chapter will focus on the fundamentals of SEO applied to content, helping you increase the visibility of your content and, consequently, attract more traffic to your website.

UNDERSTANDING SEO

SEO involves a series of techniques and practices designed to improve the position of your pages in the search results of search engines such as Google. The goal is to make your content as visible as possible to those who are searching for topics related to what you offer.

KEYWORDS: THE HEART OF SEO

Choosing appropriate keywords is crucial to your SEO success. Keywords are the terms that users type into search engines when looking for information.

1. **Keyword Research:** Use tools like Google Keyword Planner, Ahrefs, or SEMrush to find relevant keywords that your target audience is using.
2. **User intent:** Understand the intent behind your audience's searches. This will help create content that answers their questions or needs.
3. **Use of keywords:** Integrate these keywords naturally into your titles, subtitles, meta tags and throughout the content.

ON-PAGE OPTIMIZATION

On-page optimization refers to all the measures you can take directly within your website to improve your position in search engines:

1. **Titles and descriptions:** Make sure each page has a unique title and meta description that includes your target keywords.

2. **URL Structure:** Use clear URLs that include relevant keywords.
3. **Heading Tags:** Organize content using heading tags (H1, H2, H3) to help search engines understand the structure of your content.
4. **Internal links:** Incorporate links to other pages on your website to help increase site dwell time and improve the indexing of your pages.

OFF-PAGE OPTIMIZATION

SEO isn't limited to what's on your website. Off-page optimization is equally important:

1. **Backlinks:** Getting links to your website from other reputable sites can significantly improve your authority and search rankings.
2. **Social media:** Presence and activity on social media can help increase the visibility of your content and generate more traffic to your website.

ANALYSIS AND ADJUSTMENT

SEO optimization is an ongoing process. It's essential to monitor your content's performance through tools like Google Analytics and adjust your strategy as needed:

1. **Monitor traffic:** See which pages attract the most visitors and which keywords are performing best.
2. **Content adjustment:** Regularly update content to maintain its relevance and improve your rankings.

By mastering the SEO fundamentals detailed in this chapter, you will be well positioned to increase your content's online visibility, attracting more qualified visitors and ultimately converting them into customers.

In the next chapter, we will dive into persuasive writing techniques that can turn your readers into desired actions.

PERSUASIVE WRITING

Persuasive writing is an essential tool for any content creator who wants to encourage readers to take specific actions. This chapter will equip you with writing techniques that can transform your texts into powerful conversion media, helping you achieve your business goals more effectively.

UNDERSTANDING PERSUASIVE WRITING

Persuasive writing is the strategic use of words to convince someone to agree with your idea or take a specific action. In the context of content marketing, this means creating copy that motivates readers to make a purchase, sign up for a service, attend an event, or any other goal your campaign wants to achieve.

KEY ELEMENTS OF PERSUASIVE WRITING

1. **Know your audience:** Before writing, deeply understand who your readers are, what they value, and what their needs and desires are.
2. **Clarity in the message:** Your message must be clear and direct. Avoid ambiguity and be specific about what you are offering and what you expect in return.
3. **Appeal to emotions:** People are often motivated by emotions, not just logic. Use stories, metaphors, and emotional language to connect on a deeper level.
4. **Use social proof:** Incorporating testimonials, case studies and expert opinions helps build credibility and trust in your message.
5. **Strong Calls to Action (CTAs):** Each piece of content should include a clear CTA, encouraging the reader to take the next step. Be creative and direct with your CTAs to maximize conversion rates.

PERSUASION TECHNIQUES

- **Principle of reciprocity:** Offer something of value before asking for something in return. This could be useful information, free tips, or access to exclusive

resources.
- **Consistency and commitment:** Once someone agrees to a small request, they are more likely to agree to larger requests in the future.
- **Social proof:** People tend to do things they see other people doing. Show that other people trust your brand or have benefited from your products.
- **Authority:** Show that you are an expert in your field through the use of well-researched, informative content.
- **Scarcity and urgency:** Limiting the availability of an offer or emphasizing that it is a limited-time opportunity can encourage quick action.

PUTTING PERSUASIVE WRITING INTO PRACTICE

To truly master persuasive writing, practice regularly and analyze the effectiveness of different approaches. Test multiple versions of your content to see what resonates best with your audience and adjust as needed.

By the end of this chapter, you should feel more confident in your persuasive writing abilities. The techniques presented here will help you create content that not only informs, but also inspires and motivates readers to take action.

In the next chapter, we'll explore how storytelling can be integrated into your content to make it even more engaging and memorable.

STORYTELLING IN CONTENT

Storytelling is one of the most powerful tools in content marketing. Stories connect people, evoke emotions, and are memorable, which can transform your content from informative to inspiring. This chapter explores how to use effective storytelling to make your content more engaging and memorable, helping you build a deeper relationship with your audience.

THE POWER OF STORYTELLING

Stories have the power to capture people's attention in a way that isolated facts and data often cannot. They can make your content more relatable and help convey complex messages in a more digestible way. In the context of marketing, storytelling is used to:

1. **Humanize your brand:** Telling stories about the people behind your company or the customers who benefit from your services creates a personal connection with your audience.
2. **Reinforce brand message:** Stories that reflect your company's values and mission can strengthen brand identity and promote customer loyalty.
3. **Increase engagement:** Stories are more likely to generate an emotional response, encouraging comments, shares, and other forms of interaction.

ELEMENTS OF A GOOD STORY

For a story to be effective, it must include certain key elements:

1. **Characters the audience can identify with:** Whether it's a customer, an employee, or even yourself, choose characters that reflect your audience.
2. **A conflict or challenge:** Every good story has a point of tension that keeps the audience interested.
3. **A satisfying resolution:** Show how your product or service can solve challenges or help characters achieve their goals.
4. **Clear lessons:** Make it clear what the audience can learn

from the story.

IMPLEMENTING STORYTELLING IN CONTENT

Here are some practical tips for integrating storytelling into your content strategy:

1. **Use customer success stories:** Narratives about how your products or services have helped real customers are incredibly persuasive.
2. **Tell your brand's story:** Share your company's journey, the challenges faced and how they were overcome.
3. **Incorporate narrative elements into different content formats:** From blog posts to videos, use storytelling structure to shape your content.

TIPS FOR EFFECTIVE STORYTELLING

- **Be authentic:** The best stories are those that are true. Don't exaggerate or invent elements that could undermine your audience's trust.
- **Be specific:** Specific details enrich your story and make it more credible and vivid.
- **Use emotions:** Emotions are the key to connecting with the audience. Determine what emotion you want to evoke and build your story around it.

By the end of this chapter, you should be able to use storytelling to make your content not only more interesting, but also more effective in creating a lasting connection with your audience.

Ready to take your content to the next level with advanced optimization and formatting techniques? In the next chapter, we'll explore best practices for formatting and optimizing your content for easy reading and maximum engagement.

CONTENT OPTIMIZATION AND FORMATTING

The way your content is presented can significantly impact its effectiveness. This chapter discusses best practices for formatting and optimizing your content, making it not only visually appealing but also easy to read and engaging. Let's explore how small changes to your presentation can increase clarity and keep your audience interested from start to finish.

THE IMPORTANCE OF FORMATTING

Good formatting helps guide the reader through your content in a fluid and intuitive way. Well-formatted text is easier to scan and allows readers to quickly find the information they are looking for. This not only improves user experience, but can also increase page dwell time, which is beneficial for SEO.

EFFICIENT FORMATTING ELEMENTS

1. **Headers and subheaders:** Use these to break text into digestible sections. They should be clear and informative, indicating what the reader will find in the next section.
2. **Short Paragraphs:** Keep your paragraphs short and focused. Dense text can discourage reading, especially on mobile devices.
3. **Lists and points:** Numbered or bulleted lists are great for summarizing information or presenting multiple points in a clear and organized way.
4. **Bold and italics:** Use these resources to highlight important keywords or concepts, but in moderation so as not to overload the text.
5. **Internal and external links:** These not only improve SEO but also provide additional resources for readers who want to explore topics in more depth.

CONTENT VISUAL OPTIMIZATION

The visual aspect of your content is crucial. Images, videos, and other graphics can significantly enrich the user experience and help explain complex concepts more effectively.

1. **Relevant images:** Use images that complement and reinforce the text. Make sure they are high quality and properly licensed.
2. **Infographics and diagrams:** These are excellent for representing data or processes in a visual and easy-to-understand way.
3. **Videos:** Embedding videos can significantly increase engagement. Make sure they are professional and relevant to the content.

ACCESSIBILITY AND RESPONSIVITY

Ensuring your content is accessible and responsive is key. This means it must be easily accessible and readable on a variety of devices and screen sizes.

1. **Test on different devices:** Regularly check how your content appears on smartphones, tablets and desktops.
2. **Use of Alt Text in images:** This improves accessibility for people with visual impairments and also helps with SEO optimization.
3. **Responsive design:** Ensure your website or blog has a responsive design that automatically adjusts to provide the best experience on any device.

Carefully formatting and optimizing your content not only improves readability but also the overall effectiveness of your communication. By applying these practices, you will ensure that your content not only attracts attention, but also retains interest and engages your audience efficiently.

Ready to expand the reach of your content? In the next chapter, we'll discuss effective content distribution strategies to ensure your messages reach the right audience at the right time.

CONTENT DISTRIBUTION

Once you've created high-quality content and optimized it to be visually appealing and easily accessible, the next step is to ensure it reaches your target audience. This chapter covers effective content distribution strategies, helping you maximize the reach and impact of your messages.

UNDERSTANDING DISTRIBUTION CHANNELS

Choosing the right distribution channels is crucial to the success of your content marketing strategy. Each channel has its own characteristics and can reach the public in different ways. Key channels include:

1. **Social media:** Platforms like Facebook, Instagram, Twitter, and LinkedIn are excellent for sharing content and engaging with the public.
2. **Email marketing:** Sending content directly to your subscribers' inbox can be extremely effective in maintaining engagement and fostering relationships.
3. **Blogs and websites:** Publishing on your own website or blog is essential for attracting organic traffic through SEO.
4. **Partnerships and guest posting:** Collaborating with other brands or blogs can expand your reach to new audiences.

DISTRIBUTION STRATEGIES

For each type of content, there are specific strategies that can be employed to increase its visibility and effectiveness:

1. **Publication planning:** Define a publication schedule that maintains a regular frequency, appropriate to your audience's habits.
2. **Audience segmentation:** Tailor and personalize your content for different segments of your audience to increase relevance and engagement.
3. **Use of automation tools:** Tools like Hootsuite or Buffer

can help with scheduling social media posts, ensuring consistent and efficient distribution.

MEASURING DISTRIBUTION SUCCESS

Evaluating the performance of your distribution strategies is essential to understand what works and what needs to be adjusted. Some important metrics include:

1. **Reach and impressions:** How many people are seeing your content?
2. **Engagement:** How many interactions (likes, shares, comments) is your content receiving?
3. **Clicks and conversions:** How many people are clicking on the provided links and taking desired actions?

PRACTICAL TIPS

- **Repurpose content:** Transform a single piece of content into multiple formats for distribution across different channels. For example, a blog post can be converted into a video, a podcast, or a series of social media posts.
- **Encourage sharing:** Make it easy for your audience to share your content by including clear sharing buttons and calls to action.
- **Monitor trends:** Be aware of changes on social media platforms and adjust your strategies as needed to maintain relevance.

By the end of this chapter, you should have a clear understanding of how to distribute your content effectively to reach and engage your audience. Ready to further expand the impact of your content on social media? In the next chapter, we'll explore specific strategies for content marketing on social media platforms, helping you deepen relationships with your audience and expand your digital reach.

CONTENT MARKETING ON SOCIAL MEDIA

Social media is a powerful platform for content marketing, providing a unique opportunity to interact directly with your audience and amplify the reach of your message. In this chapter, we'll explore how to use social media to optimize and deepen the impact of your content.

UNDERSTANDING THE POTENTIAL OF SOCIAL MEDIA

Each social media platform has its own characteristics that can be leveraged for different types of content and marketing strategies:

1. **Facebook:** Great for building communities and sharing varied content, from text to videos and images.
2. **Instagram:** Ideal for visually appealing content, stories and direct interactions with the public through comments and stories.
3. **Twitter:** Excellent for quick updates, direct dialogue with followers and participating in current conversations through hashtags.
4. **LinkedIn:** The perfect platform for professional and business content, ideal for networking and sharing professional articles and insights.

EFFECTIVE SOCIAL MEDIA STRATEGIES

When using social media for content marketing, consider the following strategies:

1. **Personalized content:** Adapt your content for each platform, considering each platform's format and style preferences.
2. **Interactivity:** Encourage audience participation with questions, polls and calls to action that drive engagement.
3. **Frequency and consistency:** Maintain a regular presence on your chosen platforms to keep your audience engaged and interested.

LEVERAGING USER GENERATED CONTENT

User-generated content (UGC) is extremely valuable as it increases your brand's authenticity and encourages more interactions:

- **Encourage your followers to share their own stories** related to your brand or product.
- **Run contests and campaigns** that motivate users to create content that can be shared on their social networks.
- **Feature users' content** on your own pages, showing that you value their contributions.

MEASURING IMPACT

To understand the success of your social media strategies, it's crucial to monitor specific metrics:

- **Engagement:** Track likes, comments, shares and mentions.
- **Reach:** Measure how many people are being reached by your content.
- **Referred traffic:** Observe how many visitors are directed to your website through social media.

RECOMMENDED PRACTICES

- **Use high-quality images and videos** to capture attention and improve engagement.
- **Stay up to date** with changes to platform algorithms to adjust your strategies as needed.
- **Actively interact with your audience** by responding to comments and messages to build lasting relationships.

By mastering these techniques, you will be able to use social media not just as a distribution channel, but as a powerful engagement and brand-building tool.

In the next chapter, we'll explore how to effectively measure the success of your content through detailed metrics and analytics.

MEASURING CONTENT SUCCESS

Once your content is created and distributed, the next crucial step is measuring its success. This chapter covers how to use metrics and analytics to evaluate the effectiveness of your content, allowing you to make informed adjustments and optimize your content marketing strategies for even better results.

THE IMPORTANCE OF CONTENT ANALYSIS

Evaluating the performance of your content is essential to understanding what resonates with your audience and what can be improved. Without this analysis, you would be operating in the dark, not knowing which efforts are truly contributing to your business goals.

KEY METRICS TO MEASURE SUCCESS

1. **Reach and impressions:** Measure how many people saw your content, providing an idea of your visibility potential.
2. **Engagement:** Includes likes, comments, shares, and other interactions that indicate how engaging your content is.
3. **Clicks:** The number of clicks on links contained in your content can indicate the level of interest in learning more or taking a specific action.
4. **Conversion rate:** Shows how many users who interacted with your content actually performed the desired action, such as filling out a form or making a purchase.
5. **Retention:** Your content's ability to keep audiences coming back for more, an indication of long-term relevance and value.
6. **ROI (return on investment):** Evaluates the efficiency of the content in terms of financial return compared to the cost of production and distribution.

ANALYSIS TOOLS

Several tools can help analyze your content:

- **Google Analytics:** Excellent for tracking website traffic, user behavior, and conversions.
- **Social media tools:** Platforms like Facebook Insights and Twitter Analytics offer detailed data on how content is performing on these networks.
- **SEO Tools:** Tools like SEMrush and Ahrefs are useful for analyzing keyword performance and content visibility in search engines.

CREATING EFFECTIVE REPORTS

Compiling your data into clear, understandable reports is crucial to communicating the results of your strategies. Include:

- **Performance overview:** Summary of key metrics and what they tell you about the success of your content.
- **Insights and trends:** Analysis of patterns or trends that can inform adjustments to your strategies.
- **Action recommendations:** Based on the data, what are the next steps to improve the performance of your content.

USING DATA FOR CONTINUOUS IMPROVEMENT

Based on the analysis, identify areas for improvement and test new approaches to see how they impact metrics. For example, if certain types of content have high engagement but low conversion, consider adjusting the calls to action or content offered.

By the end of this chapter, you should have a solid understanding of how to measure and interpret the success of your content. With this information, you can continually refine your strategies to maximize the impact and effectiveness of your content marketing.

Ready to explore more about how content can be directly used to generate leads?

In the next chapter, we'll dive deeper into content lead generation strategies, helping you turn your audience into qualified leads and customers.

LEAD GENERATION
WITH CONTENT

Lead generation is an essential component to any successful content marketing strategy, especially for businesses that rely on continuous conversion of new customers. This chapter covers how you can use your content to capture information from potential customers and turn them into qualified leads for your business.

UNDERSTANDING LEAD GENERATION

Lead generation involves collecting information from individuals interested in your products or services and then engaging them with targeted communications. The goal is to guide them through the sales funnel until they are ready to make a purchase.

CONTENT STRATEGIES FOR LEAD GENERATION

1. **High-value content:** Offer e-books, whitepapers, or webinars that require filling out a form to access. This content must provide meaningful insights that justify the information exchange.
2. **Optimized landing pages:** Create landing pages that are optimized for conversion, focusing on highlighting the benefits of your offering and including a simple form for collecting information.
3. **Clear and visible CTAs:** Include clear calls to action (CTAs) in your content, directing users to your landing pages. Make sure these CTAs are attractive and visible to maximize click-through rates.
4. **Segmentation and personalization:** Use demographic and behavioral information to personalize your content and offers, increasing relevance and conversion likelihood.

USING LEAD CAPTURE FORMS

Forms are a vital tool in generating leads. Here are some tips for optimizing your forms:

- **Keep it simple:** Limit the number of fields on the form

so as not to discourage users.
- **Offer something in return:** Ensure that the value of what is being offered is perceived as greater than the "expense" of providing your information.
- **A/B Testing:** Try different versions of your form to see which converts best.

BEST PRACTICES FOR LEAD NUTRITION

Once you've captured leads, it's crucial to engage them with targeted content that moves them further down the sales funnel:

- **Segmented email marketing:** Send emails that continue to educate your leads about your products or services and encourage them to take the next step.
- **Personalized follow-up:** Use the information collected to personalize follow-up, increasing the relevance and effectiveness of your communications.
- **Monitoring and optimization:** Track the performance of your nutrition campaigns and adjust your strategies based on the results.

Lead generation is more than just collecting email addresses; it's about building an ongoing relationship. By creating valuable content that resonates with your audience and making it easy to capture information with effective forms and CTAs, you can turn your content into a powerful lead generation tool.

In the next chapter, we'll explore how you can repurpose your existing content to maximize return on investment by extending the lifespan of your content and reaching new audiences.

CONTENT REPURPOSING

Content reuse, or content repurposing, is an effective strategy for maximizing return on marketing investment by expanding the lifespan of existing content and reaching new audiences with minimal additional effort. This chapter explores how you can adapt, reuse, and revitalize your content for different formats and platforms.

UNDERSTANDING CONTENT REPURPOSING

Content repurposing is not simply reposting the same content on different platforms. It involves modifying, expanding, or reshaping existing content so that it fits into new contexts or meets new audience needs.

ADVANTAGES OF REPURPOSING

1. **Expanding your reach:** Different content formats appeal to different types of audiences and adapt to different platforms, helping you reach a wider audience.
2. **Message reinforcement:** By presenting the same message in different forms, you reinforce your message and increase the chances of audience retention.
3. **Saves time and resources:** Leveraging existing content saves resources that would otherwise be spent on creating new content from scratch.

EFFECTIVE REPURPOSING STRATEGIES

1. **blog posts into infographics:** A detailed post can be summarized into a visually appealing infographic ideal for sharing on social media.
2. **Create podcasts from articles:** Popular articles can be converted into podcast episodes, providing a way to reach those who prefer auditory content.
3. **Develop webinars based on e-books:** Use the detailed material from an e-book to create an interactive webinar that can directly engage with the audience.
4. **Produce videos from posts:** Convert informative posts

into tutorial or explanatory videos that can be shared on YouTube or other video platforms.

TIPS FOR EFFECTIVE REPURPOSING

- **Identify high-performing content:** Focus on reusing content that has proven to be popular and effective.
- **Adapt to the audience and platform:** Make sure that the repurposed content is adapted to the preferences of the new target audience and the characteristics of the chosen platform.
- **Stay relevant:** Update content with recent information to ensure it remains current and relevant.
- **Respect copyright and brand consistency:** When transforming content, continue to respect copyright and maintain consistency with your company's voice and brand.

Content reuse is a strategic approach that not only expands your marketing reach but also reinforces your brand message across multiple platforms and formats. By implementing the strategies discussed, you can effectively increase the lifespan of your content and reach new audiences with a considerably smaller investment.

Ready to continue exploring techniques to maximize engagement with your audience? In the next chapter, we'll discuss methods for encouraging engagement and interaction through your content, a crucial key to building a loyal community around your brand.

ENGAGEMENT AND INTERACTION

Fostering engagement and interaction with your content is vital to building an engaged and loyal community around your brand. This chapter explores techniques for encouraging your followers to interact more deeply with your content, which can improve the visibility and effectiveness of your content marketing strategies.

THE IMPORTANCE OF ENGAGEMENT

Engagement not only helps strengthen the relationship between brand and customer, but also increases the visibility of your content in social media algorithms and search engines. A high level of interaction indicates that your content is relevant and valuable, attracting more views and shares.

STRATEGIES TO INCREASE ENGAGEMENT

1. **Interactive content:** Use interactive quizzes, polls, and infographics to actively engage users. These tools encourage participation and can provide valuable data about your audience's preferences.
2. **Comments and discussions:** Encourage comments on your posts and participate in discussions. Responding to comments in a timely manner shows that you value your audience's opinion and helps build an active community.
3. **User-generated content:** Promote campaigns that encourage your followers to create and share content related to your brand. This not only increases engagement, but also provides free, authentic content that can be used across your platforms.
4. **Stories and lives:** Use the stories and live broadcasts functions on social media to connect in real time with your audience, which can generate meaningful and immediate interactions.

TECHNIQUES TO KEEP THE AUDIENCE INVOLVED

- **Content consistency:** Maintaining a regular publishing

schedule helps keep your brand in the public's mind. Consistency generates expectations and consumption habits among your audience.
- **Added value:** Constantly offer content that educates, entertains or solves problems. Added value is essential to keep the public interested and engaged.
- **Format diversification:** Switch between different content formats like text, video, image and audio to maintain interest and meet your audience's varied preferences.

MEASURING ENGAGEMENT

To evaluate the effectiveness of your engagement strategies, monitor metrics such as:

- **Interaction rates:** Includes likes, comments and shares.
- **Dwell time:** How long visitors spend with your content.
- **Click-through rate (CTR):** The percentage of people who click on a link out of total views.

Engagement and interaction are key indicators of the health of your online community and the effectiveness of your content. By implementing the strategies discussed in this chapter, you can significantly increase audience engagement, which in turn can lead to greater brand loyalty and conversions.

Ready to take the next step in using media in your content? In the next chapter, we'll explore the importance of incorporating visual elements, like images and videos, to complement and reinforce the message of your content.

USE OF IMAGES AND VIDEOS

In the world of content marketing, images and videos play a crucial role in not only attracting initial attention but also maintaining audience engagement. This chapter focuses on how you can effectively integrate visual elements into your content to complement and enhance your messages.

THE IMPORTANCE OF VISUAL ELEMENTS

Visual elements, such as images and videos, have the power to convey information quickly and in an impactful way. They can:

1. **Increase retention:** Visual content is more easily remembered than plain text.
2. **Improve engagement:** Images and videos often result in higher interaction rates such as likes, shares and comments.
3. **Facilitate understanding:** Visual elements can help explain complex concepts more clearly and directly.

STRATEGIES FOR INTEGRATING IMAGES AND VIDEOS

1. **Quality over quantity:** Prioritize the quality of images and videos. High-quality visual content reflects professionalism and brand credibility.
2. **Relevance is key:** Make sure each image or video is directly related to the text content, reinforcing the message you want to convey.
3. **SEO Optimization:** Use alt tags on all images and optimize video titles and descriptions with relevant keywords to improve visibility in search engines.
4. **Adapt for different platforms:** Customize the size and format of videos and images for each social media platform to ensure they appear optimally in each feed.

CREATING EFFECTIVE VIDEOS

Videos are extremely effective at capturing an audience's attention. Here are some tips for creating videos that engage and inform:

- **Keep them short and to the point:** For social media, short videos tend to work best. Try to keep videos between 1-2 minutes for maximum effectiveness.
- **Include subtitles:** Many people watch videos without sound, especially on mobile devices, so including subtitles can significantly increase your reach.
- **Call to action:** Always end your videos with a clear call to action, directing viewers to the desired next step.

USE OF IMAGES TO COMPLEMENT TEXTS

Images can break up large blocks of text, making content more digestible and visually appealing:

- **Infographics:** They are great for summarizing data or explaining complex steps in a visual way.
- **High-quality images:** Use images that align with your brand's visual identity to create a cohesive experience.

Effectively integrating images and videos into your content can transform the way your audience interacts with your messages. In addition to improving aesthetics and deepening understanding, they are powerful tools for increasing engagement and visibility online.

In the next chapter, we'll explore how you can use visual content in email marketing campaigns to increase open and click rates.

CONTENT FOR EMAIL MARKETING

Email marketing continues to be one of the most effective and personal tools in digital communication strategies. Integrating valuable content into your email campaigns not only increases open and click-through rates but also strengthens relationships with your subscribers. This chapter explores how you can enrich your email campaigns with relevant visual and textual content.

THE IMPORTANCE OF CONTENT IN EMAIL MARKETING

Emails offer a direct and personal way of communicating with your audience. Unlike social media, where content is seen by everyone, an email is a more private and targeted conversation. Here are a few reasons why email content is so crucial:

1. **Personalization:** Emails allow for very precise segmentation and personalization, which can significantly increase the relevance and impact of the message.
2. **Traffic Driving:** Well-crafted emails can drive significant traffic to your website or blog.
3. **Conversions:** Through clear and effective CTAs, emails are an excellent tool for converting subscribers into paying customers.

DEVELOPING EFFECTIVE CONTENT FOR EMAIL

1. **Rich and relevant content:** Each email must add value, whether educating, informing or entertaining your subscribers. Include content that responds to the needs and interests of your audience.
2. **Using images and videos:** Images and videos can increase the engagement and visual appeal of your emails. Make sure they are optimized so as not to affect email loading speed.
3. **Responsive format:** Ensure that your emails are responsive and easy to read on any device, as a large portion of users access emails via smartphones.

EMAIL CAMPAIGNS

- **List segmentation:** Divide your email list into segments based on behavior, interests, or demographics to further personalize your messages.
- **A/B Testing:** Experiment with different subject lines, email formats, and send times to find out what works best for your audience.
- **Frequency and timing:** Find a balance in your sending frequency that keeps your audience engaged without overwhelming them.

MEASURING SUCCESS

To evaluate the effectiveness of your email marketing, consider the following metrics:

- **Open rates:** The percentage of recipients who open the email.
- **Click-through rates:** The percentage of recipients who click on a link within the email.
- **Conversions:** The number of desired actions performed from an email.

The content of your emails must be strategically designed to nurture, inform and convert your subscribers. By integrating valuable content and utilizing segmentation and personalization techniques, you can transform your email marketing campaigns into a powerful tool for achieving concrete business goals.

In the next chapter, we'll explore how to build and cultivate a community through your content, creating a solid base of loyal and engaged followers.

BUILDING COMMUNITY THROUGH CONTENT

Building a community around your brand is essential for fostering loyalty, improving engagement, and even increasing conversion. This chapter focuses on how you can use content strategically to create and cultivate a vibrant community that organically supports and promotes your brand.

THE IMPORTANCE OF A BRAND COMMUNITY

A successful brand community can provide a valuable environment where your customers and followers can interact with you and each other, share experiences, and learn more about your products or services. Additionally, an engaged community can:

1. **Provide valuable feedback:** Community members often provide insights that can help improve products and services.
2. **Increase customer retention:** A sense of belonging can increase brand loyalty.
3. **Facilitate word-of-mouth marketing:** Satisfied community members tend to share their positive experiences, attracting new customers organically.

STRATEGIES FOR CULTIVATING A COMMUNITY THROUGH CONTENT

1. **Create content that encourages interaction:** Post content that promotes discussion, such as open-ended questions, polls, and topics that encourage users to share their own stories or opinions.
2. **Utilize social media platforms:** Platforms like Facebook, Instagram, and Twitter are excellent for building communities. Also consider creating a dedicated group where members can interact more directly.
3. **Events and webinars:** Organize online events, such as webinars or lives, where community members can learn something new and interact in real time.

4. **Programs :** Encourage active participation with reward programs that offer incentives for members who regularly contribute to the community.

PROMOTING A POSITIVE ENVIRONMENT

- **Establish clear rules:** Define and communicate community rules to keep interactions respectful and constructive.
- **Be active and responsive:** Regularly participate in conversations by answering questions and interacting with community members.
- **Active moderation:** Monitor the community to prevent spam and toxic behavior, ensuring a safe and welcoming environment for everyone.

MEASURING COMMUNITY SUCCESS

To understand your community's impact on your brand, monitor:

- **Engagement:** The frequency and quality of interactions within the community.
- **Community growth:** The number of new members and their retention rate.
- **Impact on sales:** How much community activities influence sales and conversion.

A robust brand community is a valuable asset that can amplify the reach of your message and strengthen customer loyalty. By investing in content that promotes interaction and maintaining an environment of open and positive communication, you can transform your followers into an active and engaged community.

In the next chapter, we'll explore common challenges in content marketing and how to overcome them to keep your strategies effective and aligned with your company's goals.

COMMON CHALLENGES IN CONTENT MARKETING

Even with a well-planned strategy, content marketers often face challenges that can impede the success of their initiatives. This chapter explores some of the most common problems in the field and offers practical solutions to overcome them, ensuring your content strategies remain effective and aligned with your company's goals.

PRODUCTION OF CONSISTENT AND QUALITY CONTENT

Challenge: Maintaining a steady cadence of useful and engaging content can be exhausting, especially with limited resources.

Solution: Plan your content in advance using an editorial calendar. Consider hiring freelancers or utilizing user-generated content to diversify your content sources without overwhelming your in-house team.

REACH THE RIGHT AUDIENCE

Challenge: Reaching and engaging your desired audience can be difficult, especially on platforms saturated with competitors.

Solution: Utilize advanced targeting tools offered by social media platforms and search engines to target your content to the right people. Increase your understanding of your audience through surveys and direct feedback, adjusting content to better meet their needs and interests.

MEASURING RETURN ON INVESTMENT (ROI)

Challenge: Proving the real value of content marketing can be challenging, especially when the results are not immediately obvious.

Solution: Define clear success metrics from the start of your campaign. Use analytical tools to track engagement, conversions and other key indicators. Adapt your strategy based on hard data to improve ROI.

STAY UPDATED WITH SEO TRENDS

Challenge: SEO is an ever-changing landscape, and keeping your content visible in search results can be tricky.

Solution: Stay up to date with the latest SEO practices by attending webinars, following industry thought leaders, and reading relevant publications. Implement regular changes to your website and content to align with the latest trends and search algorithms.

DIFFERENTIATION IN A SATURATED MARKET

Challenge: Standing out in a market full of similar content can seem impossible.

Solution: Focus on creating a unique brand voice and produce content that highlights your unique value propositions. Consider less traditional, more creative approaches to presenting your content, such as interactive storytelling or innovative content formats.

Overcoming challenges in content marketing requires a combination of strategy, creativity and perseverance. By facing these obstacles head-on and adjusting your tactics according to your audience's needs and responses, you can ensure that your content strategy not only survives but thrives in a competitive environment.

In the next chapter, we'll explore how to optimize your content to boost sales and conversions, taking your content marketing to the next level.

CONTENT AND CONVERSION

Turning visitors into customers is the ultimate goal of many content marketing strategies. This chapter focuses on how to optimize your content to drive sales and conversions, using effective techniques that encourage users to take specific actions.

THE IMPORTANCE OF CONTENT IN THE CONVERSION JOURNEY

Content plays a crucial role at each stage of the sales funnel, helping to educate, inform and persuade potential customers. Effective content can increase brand trust and authority, removing barriers to conversion and motivating action.

CONTENT STRATEGIES TO INCREASE CONVERSIONS

1. **Content targeted at the funnel stage:** Create content that is relevant to each stage of the customer journey, from informative posts at the top of the funnel to case studies and testimonials at the bottom of the funnel.
2. **Clear, persuasive calls to action:** Include clear CTAs throughout your content, directing readers to the next step, whether that's signing up for a newsletter, downloading a guide, or making a purchase.
3. **Social proof and testimonials:** Use testimonials, reviews and case studies to build credibility and demonstrate the value of your products or services.
4. **Limited-time and scarcity offers:** Create a sense of urgency with limited-time offers or products with limited availability to encourage quick decision-making.

OPTIMIZING CONTENT FOR CONVERSION

- **A/B Testing:** Use A/B testing to try different versions of your content, page layouts, images, and CTAs to see what converts best.
- **Targeting and personalization:** Personalize your content for specific segments of your audience to

increase the relevance and effectiveness of your messages.
- **analysis** : Constantly monitor how your content is performing and use this data to optimize your conversion strategies.

MEASURING THE IMPACT OF CONTENT ON CONVERSIONS

To truly understand the impact of your content on conversions, it is essential to measure and analyze the following aspects:

- **Conversion rate:** The percentage of visitors who take the desired action after interacting with your content.
- **Average order value:** The average value of a purchase made as a result of a content conversion.
- **Cost per conversion:** How much you are spending on content marketing to get each conversion.

Content is not just a means of attracting traffic; is a powerful tool for converting that traffic into revenue. By focusing on specific strategies that leverage content to drive conversions, you can transform your marketing approach and see a significant return on investment.

In the next chapter, we will discuss the importance of maintaining authenticity and transparency in content marketing, which are essential for building trust and brand loyalty.

AUTHENTICITY AND TRANSPARENCY

In a digital world saturated with marketing in all forms, maintaining authenticity and transparency has become essential for brands that want to build lasting trust and loyalty with their customers. This chapter discusses the importance of these values in content marketing and how to incorporate them into your strategies to strengthen relationships with the public.

THE IMPORTANCE OF AUTHENTICITY

Authenticity refers to the genuineness of your brand and the honesty of the messages you convey. An authentic brand not only resonates more with its audience, but also fosters a feeling of trust and credibility, crucial factors for customer loyalty.

STRATEGIES TO MAINTAIN AUTHENTICITY

1. **Real Stories:** Use real stories from customers, employees, or even your own business experiences to connect with your audience. Avoid exaggerations and stick to the facts.
2. **Message consistency:** Ensure your communication is consistent across all channels and platforms. Sudden changes in voice or message can confuse your audience and damage your credibility.
3. **Feedback and dialogue:** Encourage and value feedback from your customers. Being open to criticism and responding constructively is a pillar of authenticity.

THE IMPORTANCE OF TRANSPARENCY

Transparency is about being open about your company's processes, policies and practices. Showing your customers and followers that your company is open and honest can be a significant competitive advantage.

STRATEGIES TO PROMOTE TRANSPARENCY

1. **Clarity in processes:** Be transparent about how your products are made or your services are performed. This

includes everything from the sourcing of materials to working practices.
2. **Clear policies:** Be clear about your policies, especially those that directly affect customers, such as privacy and return policies.
3. **Crisis communication:** If something goes wrong, such as a product error or service failure, communicate this openly to your audience and explain what is being done to correct the situation.

MEASURING THE IMPACT OF AUTHENTICITY AND TRANSPARENCY

The impact of these values can be measured through:

- **Customer engagement:** Greater authenticity and transparency often result in increased customer engagement with the brand.
- **Customer loyalty:** Look at customer retention and repurchase rates to measure the long-term impact of authenticity and transparency on customer loyalty.
- **Brand Reputation:** Monitor your brand's sentiment and mentions on social media and other platforms to assess how authenticity and transparency are impacting your overall reputation.

Authenticity and transparency are not just marketing trends, they are expectations of the modern consumer. Incorporating these values into your content marketing not only strengthens trust with your audience, but also establishes a solid foundation for sustainable growth and customer loyalty.

In the next chapter, we'll discuss the future of content marketing and explore the emerging trends that will shape the next era of this essential discipline.

FUTURE OF CONTENT MARKETING

As we move into an increasingly digitized world, content marketing continues to evolve, adapting to new technologies, changes in consumer behaviors and innovations in communications. This chapter explores the emerging trends that are shaping the future of content marketing, offering insights into how companies can adapt and thrive in this ever-changing landscape.

ARTIFICIAL INTELLIGENCE AND PERSONALIZATION

AI is revolutionizing content marketing, offering new ways to personalize the user experience at scale. AI tools can analyze user behavior data to create highly personalized content that meets individual needs, improving the effectiveness and efficiency of campaigns.

- **Practical applications:** Using chatbots to provide instant and personalized responses, recommendation algorithms to suggest relevant content, and automation to optimize content distribution.

INTERACTIVE CONTENT

Interactive content is not just more engaging; it also allows consumers to be active participants in your brand's narrative. This can include everything from quizzes and polls to augmented reality (AR) and immersive experiences that provide a deeper, more memorable connection.

- **Benefits:** Improves engagement rates, increases interaction time with the brand and provides valuable data on consumer preferences.

VIDEO AND LIVE STREAMS

Video continues to be one of the most powerful forms of content, with a growing trend toward using live video to engage audiences in real time. Social media platforms are expanding their live video capabilities, offering brands new opportunities for authentic and transparent interactions.

- **Implementation strategies:** Utilize videos for tutorials, behind-the-scenes, live events, and Q&A sessions to foster an engaged and informed community.

SUSTAINABILITY AND SOCIAL RESPONSIBILITY

As consumers become more aware of the social and environmental impacts of their purchases, they expect brands to demonstrate a commitment to sustainable and ethical practices. Content that communicates a brand's social responsibility efforts can strengthen customer loyalty and trust.

- **Approaches:** Share stories about how products are made, highlight sustainability initiatives, and engage consumers in social impact campaigns.

The future of content marketing promises an even greater integration of technology, interactivity and personalization, all aligned with a growing demand for transparency and ethics. To stay relevant and effective, brands must be willing to adapt their strategies, explore new tools and proactively respond to changing consumer expectations.

In the next chapter, we'll cover essential resources and tools for content creators that can help keep your content strategy at the forefront of innovation.

RESOURCES AND TOOLS FOR CONTENT CREATORS

For content creators to keep their strategies effective and innovative, it is essential to have the right tools. This chapter covers a selection of fundamental resources and tools that can help with the creation, distribution and analysis of content, facilitating the management of content marketing campaigns and increasing their effectiveness.

CONTENT CREATION TOOLS

1. **Canva :** A graphic design tool that is extremely useful for creating eye-catching visual images, infographics, presentations, and other types of visual content, even for those without advanced graphic design skills.
2. **Adobe Creative Cloud:** Offers a range of software for video editing, graphic design, photo editing and web design, which are essential for content creators looking for a more robust and professional solution.
3. **Grammarly:** A grammar checker that helps polish writing, ensuring content is not only grammatically correct, but also clear and concise.

CONTENT DISTRIBUTION TOOLS

1. **Hootsuite:** Allows you to manage multiple social media accounts from a single dashboard, schedule posts, monitor what is being said about your brand and analyze traffic.
2. **Mailchimp:** An email marketing automation tool that helps with creating email campaigns, segmenting contact lists, and analyzing campaign performance.
3. **WordPress :** A content management platform that allows you to easily create and manage a blog or website, with numerous plugins that help with SEO, security and other important features.

CONTENT ANALYSIS TOOLS

1. **Google Analytics:** Provides detailed data on website

traffic, user behavior and conversion, helping you measure the effectiveness of content strategies.
2. **BuzzSumo:** Allows you to analyze the most shared content on social media or by keywords, identify influencers and monitor competitors, which is crucial for adjusting content strategies.
3. **Ahrefs:** A comprehensive SEO tool that offers features for backlink analysis, keyword research, competitive analysis, and more.

Additional Resources

- **Courses and certifications:** Platforms like Coursera, Udemy and HubSpot Academy offer courses that can help improve skills in digital marketing and content marketing.
- **Webinars and workshops:** Attending webinars and workshops is a great way to stay up to date with the latest industry trends and best practices.

Equipping yourself with the right tools and resources can significantly transform the effectiveness of your content marketing strategies. By leveraging these technology solutions, you can not only save time and resources, but also gain valuable insights that will drive the success of your campaigns.

In the next chapter, we'll conclude our journey into the world of content marketing by discussing how you can create a lasting and impactful content legacy.

CREATING A CONTENT LEGACY

As we reach the end of this comprehensive guide on content marketing, it is essential to reflect on how you can not only apply the strategies discussed, but also create a legacy of content that endures and continues to positively impact your brand and your audience. This chapter covers how to keep your content strategies dynamic, innovative, and effective over the long term.

SUSTAINING GROWTH THROUGH CONTENT

1. **Continuous adaptation:** The digital world is constantly evolving, and so are consumer expectations. Stay up to date with market trends and adjust your content strategies as needed to remain relevant and effective.
2. **Constant innovation:** Don't be afraid to experiment with new content formats, emerging technologies, or unexplored strategies. Innovation is key to standing out in a competitive market.
3. **Continuous education and learning:** Encourage your team to continually seek knowledge in content marketing and related areas to improve their skills and competencies.

BUILDING LASTING RELATIONSHIPS

- **Deep audience engagement:** In addition to attracting new customers, focus on nurturing long-term relationships with your existing audience through regular communication and personalized content that meets their evolving needs.
- **Community Building:** Continue investing in building and maintaining an active community. An engaged community can be a valuable source of feedback, support, and word-of-mouth promotion.

MEASURING LONG-TERM SUCCESS

- **Performance analysis:** Use analytical tools to continuously monitor the performance of your content.

Adjust your strategies based on hard data to ensure they remain efficient and aligned with your business objectives.
- **Regular reporting:** Establish a reporting system that allows you and your team to view progress and identify areas for improvement.

LEAVING A LEGACY

- **Documentation of strategies and processes:** Create a knowledge repository that includes your strategies, processes and learnings. This not only helps with orienting new team members but also ensures continuity and efficiency of operations.
- **Corporate and social responsibility:** Consider how your brand and content initiatives can contribute to larger social issues. Brands that demonstrate genuine concern about global issues can build a legacy of respect and trust.

Creating a content legacy is not a task that can be accomplished overnight. It requires dedication, innovation and an ongoing commitment to quality and relevance. By applying the principles and strategies discussed throughout this book, you will be well equipped to develop a content marketing program that not only meets your company's current needs but also builds a solid foundation for the future.

With this, we conclude our detailed journey through the world of content marketing. I hope the strategies, tips, and insights shared here inspire and guide you on your own content marketing journey. Move forward with confidence, creativity and a focus on genuine engagement and creating value for your audience. Success in your content initiatives is within your reach.

As we turn the final page of this journey together, I sincerely hope that the learnings shared here have touched your heart and sparked new perspectives. If this book has brought you any value, I kindly ask that you take a few moments to leave a review on Amazon. Your words not only help me grow and hone my craft, but they also guide other readers in their quests for knowledge and inspiration. Your opinion is a valuable gift, both for me and for the community of readers looking for stories that transform. I sincerely thank you for sharing this journey with me and I hope we can meet again in the pages of a new adventure.

REGINALDO OSNILDO

Hello, I'm Reginaldo Osnildo, author and innovator in the areas of sales, technology, and communication strategies. My experience ranges from the academic environment, as a professor and researcher at the University of Southern Santa Catarina, to practice as a strategist at Grupo Catarinense de Rádios. With a PhD in sales narratives and digital convergence, and a master's degree in storytelling and social imaginary, I bring my readers a unique fusion of theory and practice. My goal is to provide knowledge in a simple, practical and didactic language, encouraging direct application in personal and professional life.

Yours sincerely

Reginaldo Osnildo

+55 48 991913865

reginaldoosnildo@gmail.com